A DRAWING
RETROSPECTIVE
1963–2003

ANDRZEJ JACKOWSKI

A DRAWING
RETROSPECTIVE
1963–2003

SELECTED AND
INTRODUCED BY TIMOTHY HYMAN

———

UNIVERSITY OF BRIGHTON
PURDY HICKS

PREFACE

We would like to take this opportunity to thank Andrzej Jackowski – it has been a great joy for us to have worked with him for over a decade. We would also like to thank those others who have made this exhibition so memorable: Timothy Hyman for his thoughtful and sensitive essay and the extraordinary care he has taken in the selection of the works for the exhibition; the University of Brighton for their support which has made this catalogue possible; and finally the collectors who have kindly loaned their works.

Rebecca Hicks, Frankie Rossi & Nicola Shane · Purdy Hicks Gallery

A DRAWING RETROSPECTIVE · 1963–2003

Andrzej Jackowski established a reputation as a painter almost as soon as he left the Royal College of Art in the late 1970s. His achievement as a draughtsman is less familiar, reaching further back, and falling into three main sequences. First, his apprentice years, taking him through several sharply contrasted influences, and into various blind alleys. Then, already in his thirties, his arrival at a seam of resonant imagery – in his own phrase, 'a picture of a space in which things happen'.[1] Finally, from his mid-forties, a process of paring-down and concentration: 'trying to find it all in one image'.[2]

His range of medium could suggest the virtuoso: not only pencil, water-colour, crayon, etching, charcoal, pen and ink, but also bitumen and oil pastel (sometimes thinned with turps to rub in tone); with any or all of these deployed in combination. Yet his drawing activity has always remained essentially private. Few of these sheets have been exhibited, and all but four remain still in the artist's possession. Their function ranges widely, from the excited first notation of an idea, to the study made to salvage a picture half-shipwrecked, to the watercolour or print that rephrases in graphic terms a large painting already completed.

In Britain, through much of the period covered by this show, drawing has been a neglected art. Neither our National Gallery nor our two Tates give room to works on paper, and there are few prominent public spaces where a contemporary drawing exhibition is likely to be held. (There has been no London equivalent, for instance, to New York's admirable Drawing Center on Wooster Street.) Yet one fine recent exhibition opening in London around the same time this project was conceived, might serve as model. Devoted to Carlo Carrà (the Italian 'metaphysical' artist Jackowski has long admired), it superbly vindicated the concept of the 'drawing retrospective'. At the Estorick Foundation, we were able to grasp the entire development of this complex artist, but in two rooms. Each of Carrà's key images was in place, at the moment of its first discovery, yet each abbreviated, compressed. One watched a lifetime unfolding as a series of linear signs.

11 *Tantric Rooms*
1974 · gouache · 11.7 × 12 cm

Jackowski's Polish parents met in the Red Cross at the battle of Monte Cassino, arriving in Britain in the aftermath of war. In 1947, he tells us, 'I was born in a Polish hospital in North Wales. For the next eleven years, the three of us lived in a camp for refugees near Crewe. The huts in the camp were made of wood covered in tar.'[3] Throughout those years in the camp, Jackowski's first and main language was Polish. The sense of being an alien, an exile, displaced from a lost nation – a land of forest, snow and Baltic shore – permeated the child's consciousness. Eventually the family come to west London. The boy was enrolled at Holland Park Comprehensive, where his work in the artroom or beyond first became of absorbing interest. But this activity was always bound up with a personal quest, for some image of wholeness, beyond all loss and fragmentation. 'When I was about fourteen, my parents separated. About the same time, I painted a self-portrait, and made a decision to become a painter.'[4]

Just enough survives to plot a development. Several emphatic little images made in soft pencil as a sixteen-year-old schoolboy show an exceptional graphic confidence. A football stadium in reddish pastel reveals a gift for creating atmospheric space. Two grey gouaches represent his foundation year at Camberwell School of Art – a strict, liferoom-centred regime; 'drawing an egg for a week, that kind of thing'.[5] Under Euan Uglow he measured in the approved 'Camberwell dot-and-carry' manner, a drawing system he would later struggle to unlearn. His passing on to Falmouth, in 1967, coincided with the apogee in British art schools of American colour-field painting. 'There was this feeling that you were not allowed to tell stories in painting. There was abstraction and only abstraction.'[6] Thwarted, he began in his second year to make films: 'very simple … little things happening, the camera panning round, discovering objects in the half-light … '[7] But he wasn't painting. Understandably, he was asked to leave the course.

He'd already met his first wife, the poet Nicki Jackowska. Together, they moved to Zennor, where he worked on a farm. 'It was a pretty depressing time.'[8] Nevertheless, these Cornish years – from which few drawings survive – were crucial to his formation. 'When I got chucked out of art school, I had to

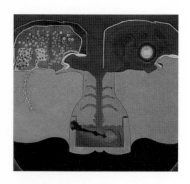

Fig.1 *Tree of Life*
1973 · oil on canvas · 132 × 132cm
Artist's collection

Fig.2 *Room with a View*
1975 · oil on canvas · 156 × 132cm
University of Liverpool Art Gallery
and Collections

really think through: "why do images"?'[9] At Falmouth one mentor was the
poet Peter Redgrove; Jackowski came to recognise that 'poetry was a way of
getting at your Self: one of the ladders for getting inside'.[10] Shouldn't drawing
also be 'a way of getting at your Self'? Visiting London in Autumn 1971, he
saw the *Tantra* exhibition at the Hayward Gallery. In Tantric art, image-
making, sexuality, and healing were all indissolubly entwined; for Jackowski,
it opened up a project of 'meditating on images as a way of knowledge'. The
vertical tree of *Tantric Thoughts* is based on a diagram of the Subtle Body,[11]
though it also has something to do with the surrealist game of 'Exquisite
Corpses', to which Redgrove had introduced him.

Up to this point, Jackowski had preserved 'an anti-intellectual attitude
towards art'.[12] Admiring the directness of child art, and also partly 'to break
the Camberwell thing',[13] he'd been drawing for several years only with his
left hand.[14] Even when he began to work more purposively, first back at
Falmouth, then at the RCA, his idiom was still close to child art. A sequence
of etchings and watercolours made over a two-year period plays on the
figure-in-an-enclosure: Beast, or Naked Girl, framed in the rectangle of
Window, Door, or Bed. In *Room with a View*, the grey woman is splayed
against the red fields of bed and carpet; the 'view', as becomes explicit a year
later, is that of ourselves as voyeur, gazing in at her nakedness. Seeing an
exhibition of Howard Hodgkin at Oxford (and then meeting him at the RCA)
helped deepen this language of brightly patterned but inhabited compart-
ments. Jackowski's handling became richer, and more impassioned, with the
woman now scrawled in bitumen-black.

It was a large, oil-painted variant of this composition that was selected for
the 1976 John Moores painting competition – Jackowski's first serious public
showing. But meanwhile, at the Royal College, he'd encountered a range of
sympathetic yet essentially analytical teachers, including Peter de Francia,
R. B. Kitaj, and Philip Rawson, the curator of the *Tantra* exhibition.[15] By the
time Jackowski made the journey to Lausanne to see Dubuffet's Art Brut
collection he'd begun to question the validity of this aesthetic of autism.

Dubuffet had written of 'an irreducible antagonism between the creation of art and a desire to communicate with the world'.[16] Yet Jackowski had travelled on to Italy, seeing Giotto's Arena Chapel in Padua; and in Paris on the way back stumbling across some pictures by Balthus. Both seemed to reopen the possibility of art as 'communication', above all in their creation of pictorial space. Back in London he read Gaston Bachelard's *The Poetics of Space*.

> I got very excited … because it was to do with reverie. He talks about an album of images … they're to do with certain spaces: drawers, nests, forgotten corners under the table … an essential poetic vocabulary.[17]

At last he could see a way in which inner and outer could be fused. He began to use his right hand again, drawing directly from people, objects, places. *The Visit* presents a real room: table, chair, fireplace, mirror, and the two figures, imbedded within them. Yet what appears to be an open door behind them, turns out to signal a very specific reference; it is the left segment of Carlo Carrà's iconic landscape of 1921, *The Pinetree by the Sea*. Carrà's own rediscovery of pictorial space, after the fragmentation of Futurism, was reached via Douanier Rousseau and Giotto. It paralleled Jackowski's journey; he loved 'the mood of thinking' Carrà's images created.[18] Within a reconstructed space, wrested from the void, reverie could flower. He saw that 'painting has a stillness, an ability to plunge vertically – you can let time unfold and bloom'.[19]

This recovery of the real, the specific, meant his range of subject-matter could now be vastly expanded. His daughter Laura; the dark waters of a pier at night; an armchair; or the steep terraces of the surrounding Brighton streets – all could now provide material for his pencil. The self, large-eyed, lips parted, gazes over the curved rim of the mirror – both out and in. Suddenly he was linked to a generation (as yet mostly unexhibited) who were making a similar voyage of rediscovery. It was in 1978 that I first met him, and *Tim* is one product of our reciprocal drawing sessions. In *Cowboy*, he returns to the theme of the girl-in-a-room, but now rephrased within a domestic space, its tone flecked in with a repeated dotted mark that resembles soot, or an etcher's

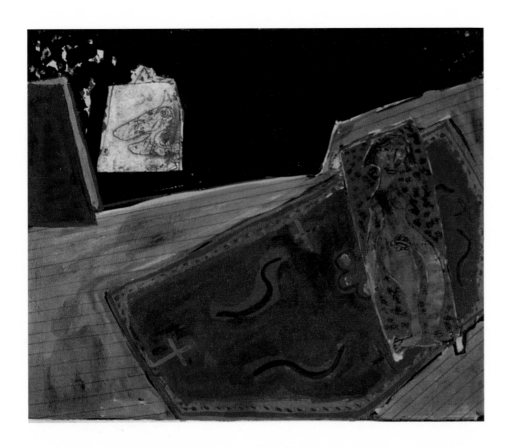

15 *Room with a View*
1975 · mixed media · 21 × 26 cm

16 *Room with a Garden*
1976 · gouache · 23.5 × 28.3 cm

20 *Woman and Fox*
1976 · mixed media · 20.2 × 18 cm

25 *First Communion*
1978 · mixed media · 34 × 27 cm

foulbite. The girl's nude back is juxtaposed to the foreground, Stetson-hatted, trumpet-blowing triumphant self. (A childhood memory from the refugee camp was his rapture at being given a cowboy-suit.) Memory might also be augmented by family snaps; the white child-self beside the altar-table of *First Communion* would in the 1990s become the subject of a whole cycle of large pictures.

He had begun to collect in albums 'found images' cut from magazines. Sometimes, almost magically, these separate sources might coalesce into a single more resonant composition, linking to his wider thought. As a reader, Jackowski was similarly fired up by what might be called 'found phrases' – such as, from Bachelard, 'Intimate Immensity'; or, from Rudolph Steiner, 'Vigilant Dreaming' – phrases that would leap out at him and provide energy for his work. He registered a special interest in magus-like figures, often from Eastern Europe. The performances of Tadeusz Kantor exercised a powerful spell; assembling props on stage and speaking *through* them, the objects emanating a life of their own. In *The Dead Class* (1976) Kantor opened a dialogue with the pre-war Polish-Jewish writer and draughtsman Bruno Schultz, invoking a crossing to some inner realm, some core of being: in Schultz's phrase, the place 'where the stories come from'. Jackowski wrote to me in 1979,

> I feel the only way to 'capture' those kinds of intimate moments … is to set traps. To construct 'vessels' to contain them. To build an ark out of furniture and prams and tables and, most important, people … [20]

A series of magus-portraits would have included *Dr Groddeck in his Clinic in Baden-Baden*,[21] and *Rudolph Steiner at Dornach*, with the founder of anthropo-sophy sculpting a figure of Christ. Steiner's emphasis on wood as a material of sacred construction linked to Jackowski's childhood in the wooden world of the camp; the dark head is set against the slant of the planks. Not only the compelling space, but the smouldering reddish-black colour, the nocturnal mood, as well as the energy of the marks – all announce that in this drawing Jackowski has indeed arrived at the core.

Fig.3 *Dr Groddeck in his Clinic in Baden-Baden*
1990 · oil on canvas · 147 × 112 cm
Artist's collection

12

AT THE LINING OF THINGS:
THE TOWER OF COPERNICUS · 1979–92

Give me your hand, take another step: we are at the roots now … on the nether side, at the lining of things, in gloom stitched with phosphorescence …

Bruno Schultz, *The Sanatorium Under the Sign of the Hour Glass* (1937)

Everything now converged upon a single decisive image. Reading about the Polish astronomer–monk Copernicus (in Koestler's *The Sleepwalkers*), he imagined him 'in his tower, living there on the Baltic Sea for thirty years with an open view of the stars at night'.[22] And this in turn 'reminded me of lying in bed as a child and trying to work out how the universe came to be, and why and when and if it would end'.[23] He had seen photos of the actual rooms where Copernicus worked (the walls still covered with geometrical diagrams). Yet if he was to conjure again those childhood thoughts – 'those awesome black hole kind of thoughts which one can suddenly tumble down into'[24] – he needed also to reconstruct the space in which they occurred. And the space-of-childhood turned out to be very specific: 'a wooden barracks covered with tar, with the inner doors made out of blankets'.[25]

Jackowski had sought for his art a special balance of outer and inner, 'turning the inner life out, as in a coat, and the outer life in'.[26] Suddenly the literal 'lining' of his childhood environment, the slatted wooden architecture, provided a metaphor, a release. He painted *The Tower of Copernicus* in three weeks, sending it almost immediately off to an open competition (the Tolly Cobbold) where it won a prize, and was promptly purchased for the Arts Council Collection. Originally the focus was to have been Copernicus himself; another Groddeck or Steiner. But the figure became, in a sense, redundant. The various objects in the room – the Wheeled Hut, the Ladder, as well as the glittering-eyed Cat-Familiar – sufficiently conjured the absent magus. Or, to put it another way, the spatial enclosure became in itself the material of reverie. The tower is felt as a kind of alchemical kitchen, already half-way to the stars, set apart from the everyday world, and joined to it only by a ladder.

He'd come across the wheeled hut in a concentration camp photograph.

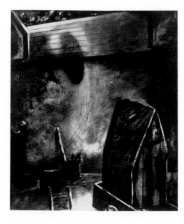

Fig. 4 *The Tower of Copernicus*
1980 · oil on canvas · 136.6 × 117 cm
Arts Council Collection, Hayward Gallery,
London

13

37 *Dr Groddeck*
1980 · mixed media · 38 × 28 cm

41 *Study for Occupations*
1981 · mixed media · 36 × 32 cm

Fig.5 *Downfalling*
1983 · oil on canvas · 167.5 × 152 cm
Collection of South East Arts, Towner
Art Gallery, Eastbourne

Fig.6 *Diving into the Wreck*
1983 · oil on canvas · 152.5 × 182.5 cm
Private collection

In the earliest pencil-study, the vertical stripes of the inmates' uniform are set against the horizontal slats. The strange gabled vehicle has ambiguous resonances: as ark-of-the-covenant; as miniature dwelling (almost a kennel); as vehicle, or half-humourous toy. 'I knew instantly when I saw the photograph of the wheeled hut that it embodied certain feelings and provided a "home" for them.'[27]

That word 'home' has a special meaning for the displaced. The shelter assembled out of flotsam corresponds to Jackowski's sense of having constructed his own precarious identity. Two years after he'd painted his first Tower, he came across an article by John Berger, 'A Home is not a House'.

> The mortar which holds the improvised home together – even for the child – is memory. Within it, tangible, visible mementoes are arranged – photos, trophies, souvenirs – but the roof and four walls which safeguard the lives within, these are invisible, intangible and biographical.[28]

Over the following decade, Jackowski would extend his wooden realm in different directions, almost as though testing its boundaries. He casts it as an upturned boat; as an ark; or as a hive. He places within it a pregnant woman, as Bride or Queen or Eve figure. He lets the seasons loose in the Tower; snow falls, then in *Downfalling* a male figure is suspended among silent flakes, while the woman looks on in stillness. (That slow-motion suspension links to the cinema of Tarkovsky, whose imagery provided a potent exemplar for Jackowski throughout the 1980s.) Partly in response to a poem by Adrienne Rich, 'Diving into the Wreck', the boat-metaphor takes another turn. Long-cherished photos of a Viking ship-burial site suddenly trigger a new imagery of *Rebuilding the City* – of an improvised society, expanding outwards from the wooden skeleton as from a hive.

So the excavated boat becomes a kind of un-burial, 'not dying, but coming alive. It felt like a womb opening, or a fruit shedding its seed.'[29] In a beautiful 1986 ink drawing, the curve of the boat thrusts upwards, within a kind of amphitheatre. (The space is, as Jackowski explained, 'archaic, mythical, but

15

Fig.7 *Settlement with Three Towers*
1986 · oil on canvas · 152.5 × 233.5 cm
Private collection

it's also Brighton, the curve of the bay as you look down on it from the racecourse'.[30]) And in *Deeds of Settlement* we are out in the ancestral Baltic forest, facing the vertical screen of close-set trees, from which the horizontal planks of childhood will eventually be constructed.

It would be wrong to think of these drawings flowing easily one from another. Jackowski has never been prolific. He sought each new image as a separate expedition, with long fallow periods between, 'times when I have to free-float'.[31] Occasionally the process seemed one of permutation – of trying out combinations of previous images, exploring possible resonances. I recall his studio as a kind of cave; a basement in the heart of Brighton, with very little natural light, but a single work on the easel, powerfully illuminated. Bruno Schultz's phrase, 'gloom stitched with phosphorescence', came to mind; and hence perhaps that quality many have commented upon, of Jackowski's forms appearing incandescent, lit from within.

Recognising a 'home' in the spaces he constructed, he felt less certain of the figures who inhabited them. It was, after all, only when Copernicus stood aside that we – spectator and painter – could step in to inhabit the space for our own purposes. Jackowski's figures and heads sometimes seemed more surrogates than protagonists. One solution was to employ a double scale – a huge head, with much smaller figures in front; or a single large figure on stage among miniature objects. In such compositions, the sense was of the figure experiencing 'past and present merged together',[32] of 'standing in your own life … with all its little images around it'.[33]

Fig.8 *The Beekeeper's Son*
1986 · oil on canvas · 168.3 × 233.7 cm
Walker Art Gallery, National Museums and
Galleries on Merseyside

In *The Beekeeper's Son*, the most ambitious of these works, a naked boy (almost life-size in the final painting) floats horizontally above a landscape. Head, hands, feet are miniscule; the expanse of stomach and thigh is centred on his erect penis. In the landscape-strip below, we can make out tiny beds; his hovering presence across the night sky seems a materialisation of their dreaming. The title is borrowed from a poem of Sylvia Plath, 'The Bee-keeper's Daughter'. He wanted the same quality of buzzing enigma.

59 Study for Vigilant Dreamer
1985 · mixed media · 39.3 × 29.5 cm

67 *Beekeeper's Head*
1991 · mixed media · 28 × 32.7 cm

All through the 1980s Jackowski's reputation had steadily grown, especially among fellow artists. In 1986 and 1989, he'd exhibited at Marlborough Fine Art (still at that time the leading London dealer for contemporary painting). When *The Beekeeper's Son* was awarded the John Moores painting prize in 1991, yet another show was hastily mounted at Albemarle Street. It marked an end, not a beginning; Jackowski and the Marlborough parted ways shortly after. He found himself experiencing a kind of revulsion towards *The Beekeeper's Son*: it was 'too fairytale', too romantic, too imbued with nostalgia. 'I wanted to make it more present.'[34] He embarked on a radical overhaul of all his most cherished aesthetic convictions.

The shift was, of course, partly that of an entire art climate. Jackowski had first come to prominence in the late 1970s, just when the foundations of modernism crumbled; when the long ascendancy of abstract painting was challenged by a renewal of imagery; when painting itself, so confidently pronounced dead, rose up again to be re-enthroned as a central medium of contemporary culture. But in the 1990s – after the art-market collapse that followed the Gulf War – that whole era appeared in a different light. Painting was seen as having colluded with Thatcherite consumerism; it became an easy target. Reviewing the John Moores exhibition, the veteran critic Tim Hilton located Jackowski's work within 'the false naivety and essential timidity of '80s yuppie painting'. In *The Beekeeper's Son*, 'nothing is defined, and indeed the merit of the painting is the way it softly changes focus every time you ask a question of it'. It is 'a continuum of evasions'.[35] Two years, earlier, Jackowski, always self-critical, had already voiced his impatience with some of his own exemplars. 'In Bachelard there isn't much feeling … it's always to do with stillness. At the present time, I'm trying to break out of that stillness.'[36] By 1992 he was resolved to strip away that beautiful 'gloom', that atmospheric murk from which his earlier imagery had emerged. One model for a new astringency, especially in drawing, was Philip Guston, who'd so bravely reinvented himself around 1970.

81 *Standing Figure*
1996 · mixed media · 96.5 × 78 cm
Private collection

83 *Standing Figure VI*
1997 · mixed media · 21 × 18.8 cm

Father and Son ⅔ AP.   A.1998.

84 *Father and Son*
1998 · etching · 27 × 32 cm

Fig.9 *Tearing Apart*
1994 · oil on canvas · 152.4 × 162.5 cm
Private collection

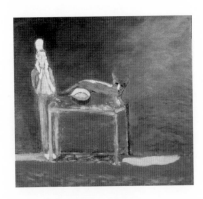

Fig.10 *A Child in the Dark*
1996 · oil on canvas · 152.4 × 162.5 cm
Artist's collection

Fig.11 *The Boy who Broke the Spell*
1996 · oil on canvas · 152.4 × 162.5 cm
Aberdeen Art Gallery & Museums Collections

The phrase 'tabula rasa' often comes to mind in connection with Jackowski's later drawings. Even if the table that stands at the centre of so many of them is in fact loaded (with a garden, a tree, a fox, a model railway, an entire city aflame) yet these images speak of clearing away, of a new nakedness. 'A table is the sign and symbol of the human', wrote Gabriel Josipovici, 'a laboratory for human making and remaking.'[37] (Hence the figure who stands at the altar-table in his long white 'laboratory-coat'.) These images resist any deep space; they are, explicitly, non-narrative, rudimentary, austere. The marks become more evidently patterned, in fields and horizontal bands of dapplings and aerated dots, filling the rectangle with a kind of effervescence.

In the 1980s Jackowski himself had remarked that his key figures were usually women. He'd identified his 'innermost being' as female: 'I'm always trying to get back to that first source. And it's feminine.'[38] But in recent years, partnered to a psychotherapist (named, as it happens, Eve) and with the birth of his young son Louis, new figures have stepped forward. Many of these are male children: the boy at play; the first communicant; the father-and-son. The spareness of these images is itself a 'dispossession', with the stage now almost emptied.

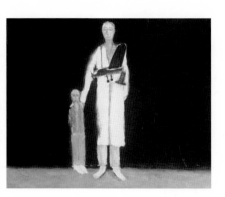

Fig.12 *Father and Son II*
1999 · oil on canvas · 152.4 × 182.9 cm
Private collection

It had been Jackowski's fate to be dealt, in childhood, a very specific experience. When he rediscovered in his thirties the imagery of the wooden barracks, it took on a resonance far larger than any autobiographical or local predicament. His drawings and paintings now became imbued with some of the defining imagery of modern European history: the concentration camps; the war and its displacement of populations; the tragic fate of Eastern Europe. Jackowski's world of wooden slats testifies to a collective experience of loss, and opens to an imagined 'Poland'. As Paul Overy (writing of Jackowski in 1986) reminds us: 'to be Polish is to have roots in a nation which has suffered repeated and concerted attempts from its neighbours to erase it from history'.[39] However personal or private Jackowski's impetus may have been in origin, he ended up, almost despite himself, creating a kind of contemporary 'history-painting'.

His own personal wounding might be centred in childhood, in family, in nationality, or in his week-to-week struggle with migraine. But from the outset, he remained convinced that image-making had a purpose connected to healing, to reparation, to becoming more whole. Interviewing him on Radio 3 in 1991, I was astonished how positively he replied to my 'impossible' question: Did he see painting as having a function? Yes, he affirmed, the making of art was not a luxury but a necessity. 'We need those kinds of transforming images like we need to dream at night.' More specifically, 'the space in the paintings allows you to dream' so that each image becomes an invitation for people 'to enter via the paintings into themselves ... to find areas in themselves which they have lost'.[40]

Jackowski's work of the 1980s spoke for a generation who had grown up under the shadow of war but had perhaps only just begun to understand how deeply it had affected our childhood. In Britain, some of the most tragic dimensions of the European experience – invasion, betrayal, civil war – had never impinged. Gabriel Josipovici (himself an alien in English culture) spoke of sensing in Jackowski's imagery 'something that for want of a better word I'd call a European quality, that I warm to'.[41] So Jackowski's special role has

Eyes for listening AP. ²⁄₃   A.5.2000

88 *Eyes for Listening*
2000 · etching · 24 × 20.5 cm

BAT. Andrzej Jackowski ~ 2003

97 *The Album*
2003 · etching · 23 × 31.5 cm

been as a reminder of, and an intermediary for, a more 'European' consciousness. His deepest affinities have lain outside contemporary English culture, and perhaps outside painting. Although he's admired artists as various as Victor Willing, Ken Kiff, Anselm Kiefer, he has identified most with the shamanistic Josef Beuys, the memory-installations of Louise Bourgeois, the dance-performances of Pina Bausch,[42] as well as with filmmakers such as Tarkovsky and Herzog.

A few months ago, I asked him whether his childhood had grown more dim. 'No,' he replied. 'Not at all. I constantly revisit it. It stands beside me in the next room, like a second habitation.'[43] That sense of intimate contact with his past is part of the thread he shares with the European figures I've listed above. For each of them, out of early memory, out of the 'timeless' dream-space generated by recollection, grows imagery that proves to be charged with an epoch's collective experience. The lyrical immediacy of Jackowski's vision is especially evident in his work on paper. This drawing retrospective establishes just how consistently his imagery has charted the consciousness of our recent past.

TIMOTHY HYMAN, 2003

ILLUSTRATED OVERLEAF
68 The Beekeeper's Son
1991 · mixed media · 69.8 × 114.5 cm

NOTES

1. Jackowski, in conversation with the author, August 2002.

2. Ibid.

3. Jackowski, in *Albums and Aliens* (catalogue, Purdy Hicks Gallery, 1997).

4. Ibid.

5. Jackowski, in conversation with the author, August 2002.

6. Gabriel Josipovici, 'A Conversation with Andrzej Jackowski', *Modern Painters*, Spring 2001.

7. Ibid.

8. Andrzej Jackowski interviewed by Timothy Hyman, *Third Ear*, Radio 3, 1991.

9. Ibid.

10. Andrzej Jackowski in conversation with Timothy Hyman, December 1988 (catalogue, Marlborough Fine Art, 1989).

11. A Nepalese chakra chart of the Subtle Body is folded into the back of the *Tantra* catalogue (Hayward Gallery, 1971).

12. Jackowski, Radio 3.

13. Jackowski, Marlborough Fine Art, 1989.

14. Tantra was classed, in terms of Indian tradition, as a 'left-hand path', avoiding the Brahmanical mainstream.

15. Rawson had already published his book *Drawing* (Oxford University Press, 1969), arguably the best analytical text on the subject ever written.

16. Dubuffet, quoted by Jackowski in 11.32 (Royal College of Art, 1977).

17. Jackowski, Marlborough Fine Art, 1989 (I have added a phrase from the Radio 3 interview of 1991).

18. Jackowski, quoted by Timothy Hyman (catalogue, Bluecoat Gallery, 1982–3).

19. Jackowski to Gabriel Josipovici in *Modern Painters*.

20. Jackowski, letter to the author, 3 June 1979.

21. Groddeck, the unorthodox psychoanalyst and author of *The Book of the It*, appealed to Jackowski partly for his ideas about the meaning of illness. 'He believed that we speak with our illness as well as with our dreams, jokes, etc.' (letter to the author, 8 February 1985).

22. Jackowski, note on *The Tower of Copernicus*, 1980.

23. Ibid.

24. Jackowski, Radio 3.

25. Jackowski, note on *The Tower of Copernicus*, 1980.

26. Jackowski, in conversation with the author, August 2002.

27. Jackowski, note on *The Tower of Copernicus*, 1980.

28. John Berger, in *New Society*, 23 June 1983.

29. Jackowski to Gabriel Josipovici, *Modern Painters*.

30. Ibid.

31. Jackowski, Radio 3.

32. Jackowski, Marlborough Fine Art, 1989.

33. Ibid.

34. Jackowski in a lecture, 2002.

35. Tim Hilton, 'Painting from Never Neverland', *The Guardian*, 23 October 1991 (Hilton was closely identified with the American-influenced abstract painters of Stockwell Depot, so prominent in the 1970s; he'd found it impossible to accept the 'refigured' painting of the 1980s).

36. Jackowski, Marlborough Fine Art, 1989.

37. Gabriel Josipovici, Introduction to *Reveries of Dispossession* (catalogue, Purdy Hicks Gallery, 1994).

38. Jackowski, Marlborough Fine Art 1989.

39. Paul Overy, 'Baltic Lyricism', *Studio International*, Autumn 1986.

40. Jackowski, Radio 3.

41. Gabriel Josipovici in *Modern Painters*.

42. Jackowski has fantasised that a dance troupe of the Bausch kind might one day employ one of his images as a starting point.

43. Jackowski, in conversation with the author, August 2002.

ANDRZEJ JACKOWSKI
A DRAWING RETROSPECTIVE
1963–2003

1 *School Drawing 1*
1963 · pencil · 9.5 × 14 cm

2 *School Drawing 2*
1963 · pencil · 9.5 × 14 cm

3 *School Drawing 3*
1963 · pastel · 9.5 × 14 cm

4 *School Drawing 4*
1963 · pencil · 14 × 9.5 cm

5 *School Drawing 5*
1963 · pencil · 14 × 9.5 cm

6 *School Drawing 6*
1963 · pencil · 14 × 9.5 cm

7 *Model I*
1967 · gouache · 29 × 21.5 cm

8 *Model II*
1967 · gouache · 28.5 × 22 cm

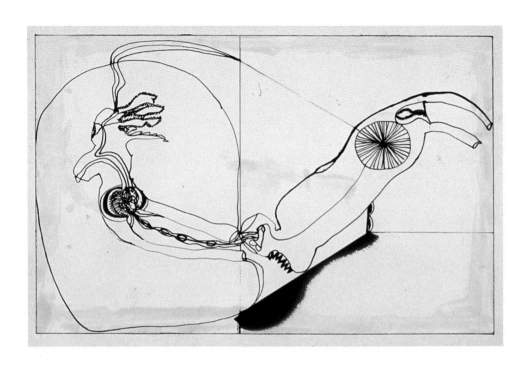

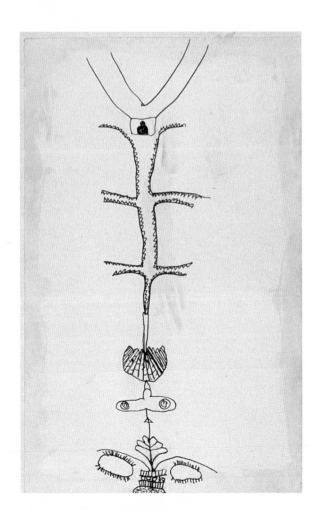

9 *The Marriage*
1973 · pen and ink · 13.7 × 22 cm

10 *Tantric Thoughts*
1973 · pen and ink · 18.5 × 11.5 cm

AP. 1/10 – The Beast.   –1975 AJ.

12 *The Beast*
1975 · etching · 20 × 24 cm

13 *Woman Dressing*
1975 · etching · 24 × 20 cm

AP. ½ – Woman with Crescent moon. —1975 AJ.

14 *Woman with Crescent Moon*
1975 · etching · 24 × 20 cm

17 *Figure in a Room*
1976 · mixed media · 25 × 26.5 cm

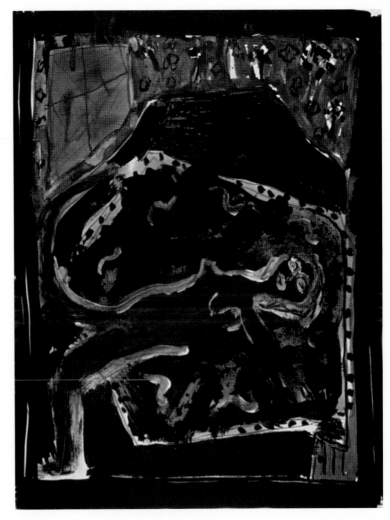

18 *Croquet*
1976 · mixed media · 26 × 19.5 cm

19 *Room with a View II*
1976 · mixed media · 27.5 × 20.5 cm

21 *Girl on a Bed*
1976 · mixed media · 20.5 × 19.3 cm

22 *The Visit*
1977 · pencil · 16 × 15 cm

23 *Self-Portrait*
1977 · pencil · 27.7 × 19.8 cm

26 *Laura*
1979 · pencil · 23 × 20 cm

24 *Two Heads*
1978 · mixed media · 30 × 61 cm

27 *Cowboy*
1979 · pencil · 19 × 27.5 cm

28 *Tim*
1979 · pencil · 27.5 × 20 cm

29 *Boscombe Pier*

1979 · pen and ink · 22.5 × 21 cm

30 *Hanover*
1979 · crayon · 31.5 × 17 cm

31 *Crossroads*
1979 · pencil · 20 × 28 cm

32 *Self-Portrait II*
1979 · bitumen · 27.7 × 20 cm

33 Chair with Cat
1979 · charcoal · 38 × 30.7 cm

34 *Chair*
1979 · crayon · 25.3 × 31.5 cm

35 *Rudolph Steiner*
1979 · mixed media · 39 × 28.5 cm

II · THE TOWER OF COPERNICUS 1979–92

36 *Copernicus*
1979 · pencil · 16 × 13 cm

38 *Study for Tower of Copernicus*
1980 · pencil · 19 × 16 cm

40 *Study for Christopher*
1981 · pencil · 23 × 17cm

39 *Study for the Tower*
1981 · charcoal · 75 × 54.5 cm

42 *Dream of Sons*
1981 · charcoal · 66 × 50.5 cm

43 *Study for the Ship's Orchestra*
1981 · mixed media · 66 × 51 cm

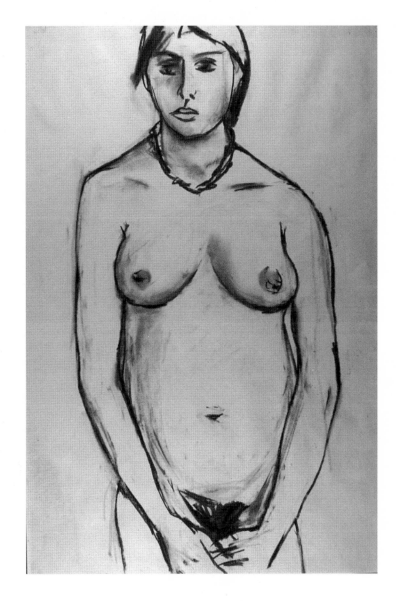

44 *Study for Salt Voyage*
1982 · charcoal · 76.2 × 55.8 cm

45 *Mother and Child*
1982 · charcoal · 76 × 54.7 cm

46 *Study for Going On*
1982 · charcoal · 84 × 59.2 cm

47 *Study for Love's Voyage*
1983 · mixed media · 50.5 × 43 cm

48 *Study for Love's Voyage II*
1983 · charcoal · 57 × 48.5 cm

50 *Diving into the Wreck*
1983 · charcoal · 71 × 50 cm

51 *Study for Downfalling*
1983 · mixed media · 74.5 × 53 cm

52 *Rebuilding the City*
1983 · charcoal · 32.5 × 46.5 cm

53 *Rebuilding the City II*
1984 · mixed media · 22.5 × 32 cm

54 *Rebuilding the City III*
1984 · mixed media · 21 × 30 cm

55 *Study for Bride*
1984 · crayon · 22.5 × 18.5 cm

56 *Study for Bride II*
1985 · mixed media · 22.5 × 21 cm

57 *Study for Black Bride*
1985 · charcoal · 40 × 35 cm

58 *The Bride*
1985 · mixed media · 51.5 × 44 cm

60 *Study for Vigilant Dreamer II*
1986 · mixed media · 21.7 × 32.3 cm

61 *Study for Vigilant Dreamer III*
1986 · mixed media · 22.6 × 32.5 cm

62 *Study for Vigilant Dreamer IV*
1986 · mixed media · 53 × 45 cm

63 *Settlement*
1986 · mixed media · 31 × 40.5 cm

64 *Deeds of Settlement No. 4*
1986 · pencil · 39.5 × 30.5 cm

66 *Touching Earth*
1990 · mixed media · 16 × 24.5 cm

65 *Eve*
1990 · mixed media · 70 × 57.5 cm

69 *Study for Beekeeper's Son II*
1992 · mixed media · 31 × 62 cm

70 *Hearing Voices III*
1992 · mixed media · 37 × 42 cm

71 *Hearing Voices IV*
1993 · mixed media · 41 × 53.5 cm

73 *Uncovered II*
1993 · crayon · 25.5 × 38 cm

72 *Uncovered*
1993 · mixed media · 18 × 24.5 cm

74 *Beneath the Tree IV*
1994 · charcoal · 26 × 33 cm

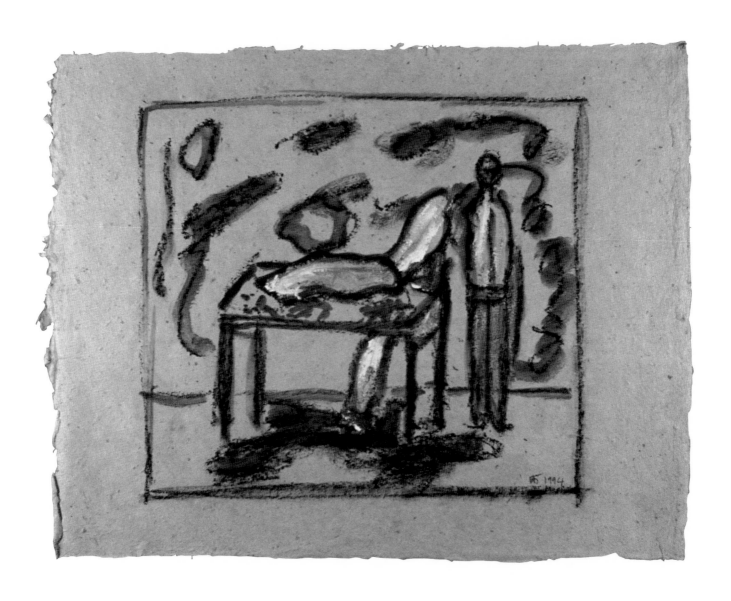

75 *A Body of Work II*
1994 · mixed media · 32 × 36.5 cm

76 *Dream*
1995 · mixed media · 41.5 × 53 cm

77 *Father and Son*
1995 · mixed media · 28 × 37 cm

78 *City Aflame*
1995 · mixed media · 26 × 31.5 cm

79 *The Assistant I*
1995 · mixed media · 56 × 42 cm
Collection Deutsche Bank AG

80 *The Assistant II*
1996 · mixed media · 52 × 41 cm
Collection Deutsche Bank AG

82 *Standing Train*
1996 · mixed media · 27 × 32 cm
Private collection

Standing train ⅔ AP.   AJ.1998.

85 *Standing Train*
1998 · etching · 27 × 32 cm

Standing Figure ⅔ AP.   AJ. 1998.

86 *Standing Figure*
1998 · etching · 25 × 21 cm

Mother & Son 2/3   AJ. 2000

89 *Mother and Son*
2000 · etching · 24.5 × 18.5 cm

Two Narrow beds AP 2/3   AJ 2000

90 *Two Narrow Beds*
2000 · etching · 23.5 × 32 cm

91 *Figure with Small Garden*
2001 · mixed media · 41 × 53 cm

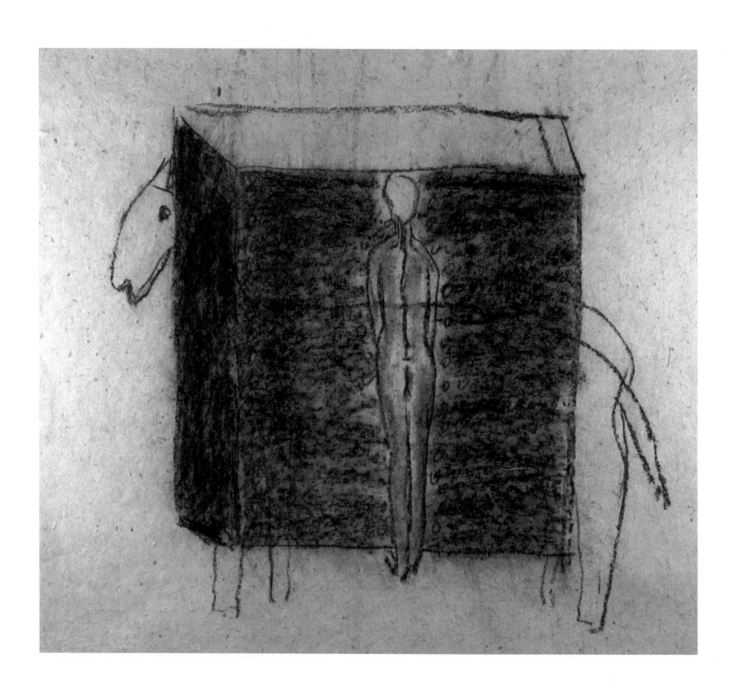

92 *Standing Figure with Wardrobe*
2002 · charcoal · 52 × 56 cm

— 93 *The Voyage*
2003 · mixed media · 41.3 × 45 cm

94 *The Voyage II*
2003 · mixed media · 29 × 35 cm

95 *The Voyage*
2003 · etching · 39 × 43 cm

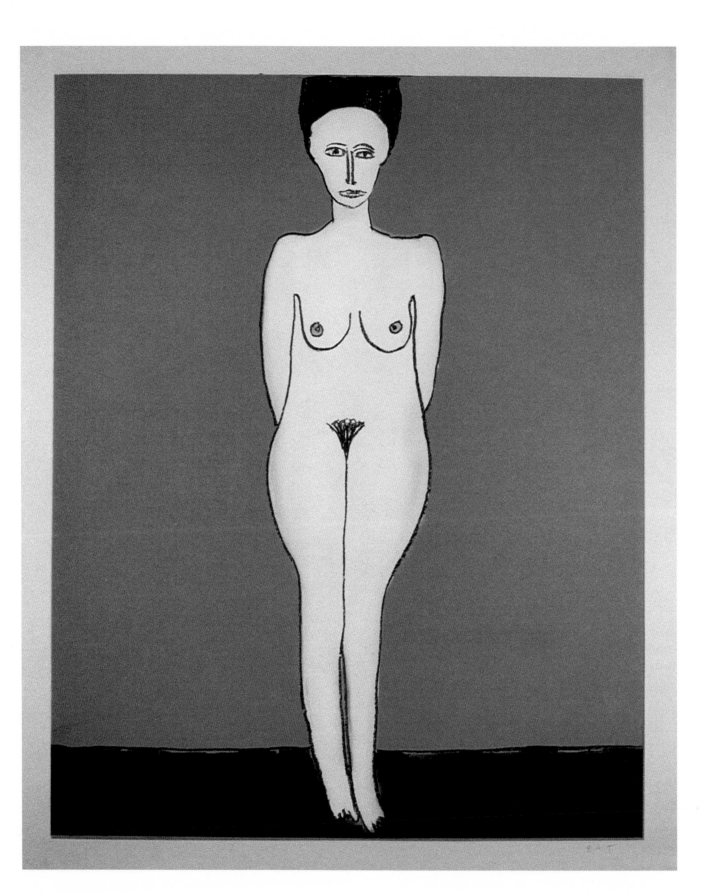

BAT. Andrzej Jackowski – 2003

96 *Woman with Her Hair Up*
2003 · etching · 76 × 61 cm

97 *The Album*
2003 · etching · 23 × 31.5 cm

LIST OF WORKS

I · THE EARLY YEARS 1963–79

Unless indicated otherwise, all works are in the artist's collection

1

School Drawing 1

1963 · pencil · 9.5 × 14 cm

2

School Drawing 2

1963 · pencil · 9.5 × 14 cm

3

School Drawing 3

1963 · pastel · 9.5 × 14 cm

Illustrated in colour on back cover

4

School Drawing 4

1963 · pencil · 14 × 9.5 cm

5

School Drawing 5

1963 · pencil · 14 × 9.5 cm

6

School Drawing 6

1963 · pencil · 14 × 9.5 cm

7

Model I

1967 · gouache · 29 × 21.5 cm

8

Model II

1967 · gouache · 28.5 × 22 cm

9

The Marriage

1973 · pen and ink · 13.7 × 22 cm

10

Tantric Thoughts

1973 · pen and ink · 18.5 × 11.5 cm

11

Tantric Rooms

1974 · gouache · 11.7 × 12 cm

Illustrated in colour on page 6

12

The Beast

1975 · etching · 20 × 24 cm

Edition of ten of which five are colour monoprints

13

Woman Dressing

1975 · etching · 24 × 20 cm

Edition of nine

14

Woman with Crescent Moon

1975 · etching · 24 × 20 cm

Edition of two

15

Room with a View

1975 · mixed media · 21 × 26 cm

Illustrated in colour on page 10

16

Room with a Garden

1976 · gouache · 23.5 × 28.3 cm

Illustrated in colour on page 10

17

Figure in a Room

1976 · mixed media · 25 × 26.5 cm

18

Croquet
1976 · mixed media · 26 × 19.5 cm

19

Room with a View II
1976 · mixed media · 27.5 × 20.5 cm

20

Woman and Fox
1976 · mixed media · 20.2 × 18 cm
Illustrated in colour on page 11

21

Girl on a Bed
1976 · mixed media · 20.5 × 19.3 cm

22

The Visit
1977 · pencil · 16 × 15 cm

23

Self-Portrait
1977 · pencil · 27.7 × 19.8 cm

24

Two Heads
1978 · mixed media · 30 × 61 cm

25

First Communion
1978 · mixed media · 34 × 27 cm
Illustrated in colour on page 11

26

Laura
1979 · pencil · 23 × 20 cm

27

Cowboy
1979 · pencil · 19 × 27.5 cm

28

Tim
1979 · pencil · 27.5 × 20 cm

29

Boscombe Pier
1979 · pen and ink · 22.5 × 21 cm

30

Hanover
1979 · crayon · 31.5 × 17 cm

31

Crossroads
1979 · pencil · 20 × 28 cm

32

Self-Portrait II
1979 · bitumen · 27.7 × 20 cm

33

Chair with Cat
1979 · charcoal · 38 × 30.7 cm

34

Chair
1979 · crayon · 25.3 × 31.5 cm

35

Rudolph Steiner
1979 · mixed media · 39 × 28.5 cm

36

Copernicus
1979 · pencil · 16 × 13 cm

37

Dr Groddeck
1980 · mixed media · 38 × 28 cm
Illustrated in colour on page 14

38

Study for Tower of Copernicus
1980 · pencil · 19 × 16 cm

39

Study for the Tower
1981 · charcoal · 75 × 54.5 cm

40

Study for Christopher
1981 · pencil · 23 × 17cm

41

Study for Occupations
1981 · mixed media · 36 × 32 cm
Illustrated in colour on page 14

42

Dream of Sons
1981 · charcoal · 66 × 50.5 cm

43

Study for the Ship's Orchestra
1981 · mixed media · 66 × 51 cm

44

Study for Salt Voyage
1982 · charcoal · 76.2 × 55.8 cm

45

Mother and Child
1982 · charcoal · 76 × 54.7 cm

46

Study for Going On
1982 · charcoal · 84 × 59.2 cm

47

Study for Love's Voyage
1983 · mixed media · 50.5 × 43 cm

48

Study for Love's Voyage II
1983 · charcoal · 57 × 48.5 cm

49

Love's Journey III
1983 · mixed media · 26.5 × 20.5 cm
Illustrated in colour as frontispiece

50

Diving into the Wreck
1983 · charcoal · 71 × 50 cm

51

Study for Downfalling
1983 · mixed media · 74.5 × 53 cm

52

Rebuilding the City
1983 · charcoal · 32.5 × 46.5 cm

53

Rebuilding the City II
1984 · mixed media · 22.5 × 32 cm

54

Rebuilding the City III
1984 · mixed media · 21 × 30 cm

55

Study for Bride
1984 · crayon · 22.5 × 18.5 cm

70

Hearing Voices III
1992 · mixed media · 37 × 42 cm

71

Hearing Voices IV
1993 · mixed media · 41 × 53.5 cm

72

Uncovered
1993 · mixed media · 18 × 24.5 cm

73

Uncovered II
1993 · crayon · 25.5 × 38 cm

74

Beneath the Tree IV
1994 · charcoal · 26 × 33 cm

75

A Body of Work II
1994 · mixed media · 32 × 36.5 cm

76

Dream
1995 · mixed media · 41.5 × 53 cm

77

Father and Son
1995 · mixed media · 28 × 37 cm

78

City Aflame
1995 · mixed media · 26 × 31.5 cm

79

The Assistant I
1995 · mixed media · 56 × 42 cm
Collection Deutsche Bank AG

80

The Assistant II
1996 · mixed media · 52 × 41 cm
Collection Deutsche Bank AG

81

Standing Figure
1996 · mixed media · 96.5 × 78 cm
Private collection
Illustrated in colour on page 20

82

Standing Train
1996 · mixed media · 27 × 32 cm
Private collection

83

Standing Figure VI
1997 · mixed media · 21 × 18.8 cm
Illustrated in colour on page 20

84

Father and Son
1998 · etching · 27 × 32 cm
Edition of twenty five
Illustrated in colour on page 21

85

Standing Train
1998 · etching · 27 × 32 cm
Edition of twenty five

86

Standing Figure
1998 · etching · 25 × 21 cm
Edition of twenty five

ANDRZEJ JACKOWSKI

1947
Born, North Wales of Polish parents

1959—66
Holland Park School, London

1966—67
Camberwell School of Art

1967—69
Falmouth School of Art

1972—73
Falmouth School of Art

1974—77
Royal College of Art

1977—2003
Lives and works in Brighton

SOLO EXHIBITIONS

1978
University of Surrey

1979
University of Surrey

1982
Moira Kelly Fine Art, London

1984
Bluecoat Gallery, Liverpool
Travelling exhibition: St Paul's Gallery, Leeds; Newlyn Art Gallery, Penzance; Dartington Hall; South Hill Park Arts Centre, Bracknell; Anne Berthoud Gallery, London

1986
Marlborough Fine Art, London

1989
Marlborough Fine Art
Gardner Centre, University of Sussex, Brighton
Castlefield Gallery, Manchester, Castle Museum, Nottingham

1992
Marlborough Fine Art

1993
Helmut Pabst Gallery, Frankfurt

1994
Reveries of Dispossession travelling exhibition: Purdy Hicks Gallery, London; Brighton Museum and Art Gallery; Ferens Museum andArt Gallery, Hull

1997
Kordegarda Gallery, National Gallery of Contemporary Art, Warsaw
Albums and Aliens: Purdy Hicks Gallery, Helmut Pabst Gallery

1999
Stored, Purdy Hicks Gallery

2000
Butler Gallery, Kilkenny
Rubicon Gallery, Dublin
White Gallery, Brighton

2002
Finding our Way, Purdy Hicks Gallery
Starr Gallery, Lewes

2003
A Drawing Retrospective 1963–2003, Purdy Hicks Gallery; travelling to University Gallery, University of Northumbria, Newcastle-upon-Tyne, and University of Brighton Gallery, Brighton

AWARDS

1978–79
South East Arts Fellowship,
University of Surrey

1981
Tolly Cobbold / Eastern Arts
Major Prize

1989
Tree of Life, Prizewinner

1990
First Prize, John Moores 17 Exhibition,
Walker Art Gallery, Liverpool

2002
Professor of Painting at the University
of Brighton

COLLECTIONS

Aberdeen Art Gallery

Arts Council of Great Britain

Atkinson Art Gallery, Southport

Bibliotheque Nationale, Paris

Birmingham City Art Gallery

British Council

British Museum

Contemporary Art Society

European Parliament, Luxembourg

Ferens Art Gallery, Hull

Fichtenbaum Foundation, Liechtenstein

Fogg Art Museum, University of
Harvard, USA

Harris Museum and Art Gallery,
Preston

Mead Gallery, University of Warwick

National Museum of Wales, Cardiff

Royal College of Art

Rugby Borough Council

South East Arts

University of Brighton

University of Liverpool

University of Surrey

Walker Art Gallery, Liverpool

ACKNOWLEDGEMENTS

The artist would like to thank Timothy Hyman for his essay and especially our dialogues and friendship over the years. The Centre for Research and Development at the University of Brighton for their support. Ray Fowler, Photographic Department, for the photographic work. And special thanks to Simon Marsh at Hope Sufferance Press for his work on the last three print projects; and to Rebecca Hicks, Frankie Rossi and Nicola Shane, Purdy Hicks Gallery, for their dedicated work and enthusiasm.

University of Brighton

Purdy | Hicks

Published on the occasion of the exhibition
Andrzej Jackowski · A Drawing Retrospective
1963–2003 by the Centre for Contemporary
Visual Art at the University of Brighton in
association with Purdy Hicks Gallery, London

Purdy Hicks Gallery
21 March – 26 April 2003

University Gallery, University of Northumbria,
Newcastle-upon-Tyne
2 May – 30 May 2003

The University of Brighton Gallery, Brighton
1 – 23 December 2003

Text © Timothy Hyman 2003
Illustrations © Andrzej Jackowski 2003

ISBN 1 873184 23 9

Designed by Dalrymple
Typeset in Albertus and Albertina
Printed by BAS Printers Ltd

Front cover illustration
One Narrow Bed [cat.87]

Back cover illustration
School Drawing 3 [cat.3]

Frontispiece
Love's Journey III [cat.49]